TROPE

FASHION
ICONS

A Celebration of Fashion's Legendary Designers

Illustrated by

DAVID LEE CSICSKO

Written by

GILLION CARRARA

CONTENTS

PAGE

IKRAM GOLDMAN

Co-founder, with her husband Josh Goldman, of iconic Chicago boutique, ikram

I was born in Israel and raised in the old city. My entire childhood, I loved my dolls and playing teacher and dressing up. I would line up all my dolls, give them names, dress them up for whatever occasion we were playing (mostly going to school) and would give them each a notepad and coloring pens. I would write their homework in the books, and I would grade it. It was a magical time in my life as there was a ton of turmoil in Israel.

My mother was diagnosed with breast cancer when I was 13 years old, and we moved to Chicago where she could get better treatment than in Israel. The kids at school were brutally mean, and I felt terribly alone. A few years later, my mother passed away and I was left on my own just before my 16th birthday. I did not know what to do or where to go, but somehow landed a job working for Joan Weinstein, the owner of Ultimo, a high-end fashion store in Chicago. There, I found my voice. I found my tribe: a group of incredibly creative and wonderful people and colleagues along with designers who graced the racks of this incredibly and meticulously curated fashion Mecca. There, I learned the power of Karl Lagerfeld's exquisite and fine workmanship, the magic of Azzedine Alaïa perfectly executed for fitting garments, and the brilliant mind of Rei Kawakubo. These are just three of the most influential designers that shaped my love of fashion.

Fast forward years later. I meet David Lee Csicsko at one of his museum shows in Chicago. On the walls hung some of the most fabulous renditions of icons from our city as interpreted through his adept hand! My first thought was that I wanted one of his pieces. More years passed and we commissioned him to do an illustration of our family which now hangs on a wall in our home. David and I have known each other personally and professionally for more than a quarter of a century. He always provides new inspiration for me in his creative vision and interpretation of iconic figures.

When he asked me to write the foreword for this book, I knew that no one could represent the incredible essence of these powerful and historic designers as he could. In looking at the images of the designers, many whom I personally knew and know, he was able to capture their humor, creativity, and whimsy. These designers helped shape periods in time that reemerge in new interpretations by new and upcoming designers. Each one of these designers plays a role in the history of fashion that trickles down in our closets and our chapters in the way we dress. I am so fortunate to be in David's orbit and to have witnessed first-hand as this wonderful book took form.

ACKNOWLEDGEMENTS

Fashion Icons is a fun look at 50 individuals who design and create remarkable clothing, where it's all about style and looking great.

Here's to David Syrek, Ron Laxamana and Dan Bowels, three of the best-dressed swells, and to Nora Csicsko Bailey and Nancy Fowler, and my friends Roger Price and Tommy Walton of Price Walton who make exquisite clothing and accessories.

And in celebration of my mother Geraldine (Gerri) Csicsko, who on her wedding day dressed chicly and sustainably. Her wedding ensemble was from a secondhand shop, an off-white wool suit with matching coat, topped off with a smart tam and pheasant feather. I've always loved a good hat!

DAVID LEE CSICSKO

I am grateful for the notes I took, the notebooks I saved, and the many lectures I documented while attending the Costume Colloquium in Florence, Italy, from 2008-2020, and the International Council of Museums. Of great help are the fashion publications I shelve, which I revisited constantly while writing these essays with the help of David Lee Csicsko and Hollis Rose Birnbaum. Among the many books I acknowledge are *Couture* by Caroline Millbanks, *Vionnet* by Betty Kirke, *Christian Dior* by Frances Muller and Oliver Gabet, *Fashion* by Charlotte Seeling, *Issey Miyake* photographs by Irving Penn, *Extreme Beauty* by Harold Koda, *Elsa Schiaparelli* by Meryl Secrest, *Mademoiselle Chanel* by C.W. Gortner, *My Bomb* by Yohji Yamamoto, and *Vivienne Westwood* by Claire Wilcox.

GILLION CARRARA

FASHION
ICONS

JEANNE-MARIE LANVIN

1867 – 1946

PARIS (FRANCE)

JEANNE-MARIE LANVIN

Versatile designer who created fashions for the entire family in her signature color, Lanvin Blue

In 1889, Jeanne-Marie Lanvin began her career as a milliner in Paris. However, it was the clothing she designed for her daughter, Marguerite, that initially gained the attraction of the Parisian upper class who requested copies be made for their own children. Soon after, she began making clothing for their mothers, cementing her place as a versatile designer of fashions for mothers and daughters of all ages, and drawing them to the atelier of her maison de couture. She also shook up the world of men's haberdashery when she opened a men's division, thus designing for the entire family.

Lanvin blurred the lines between styling day and eveningwear, making her fashions not only versatile, but also practical. Her color palette, developed in her own dye works, was critical to her success. She even developed a shade of blue that would become her signature hue: Lanvin Blue. As her business grew, she introduced fragrances, for which she is remembered to this day.

A collector of impressive works of art, her own work referenced Impressionism, Cubism, the Renaissance, and the 18th century. As a result, her textile patterns and embroideries often reflected these influences. Lanvin did not draw her original ideas, preferring to brainstorm with her staff who then interpreted her thinking on paper. They would render her bold ideas of attaching taffeta to netting, which made it appear to float, or her spiraled fabrics, giving shape to her silhouettes.

Lanvin went on to become one of the most distinguished designers of haute couture for more than 50 years. She often repeated her belief that modern clothing must have a romantic quality and not be so very mundane. Through the decades as she worked into the 20th century, Lanvin remained constant in her philosophy, embracing nature, beauty and taste as the industrial revolution and modernizing world around her transformed the lives and lifestyles of so many.

MADELEINE VIONNET

1876 – 1975

CHILLEUV-AUX-BOIS (FRANCE)

MADELEINE VIONNET

The designer who pioneered the revolutionary bias-cut dress

Young Madeleine Vionnet excelled in mathematics and became known as the "Euclid of fashion" during her working career. She worked as an apprentice seamstress beginning at the age of 12 before moving to London to work as a hospital seamstress. After securing work as a fitter, she eventually relocated to Paris, working in the fashion house Callot Soeurs. By 1912, Vionnet had established a loyal clientele and had saved enough money to be able to open her own maison de couture.

Vionnet's gowns suggested modernity, referencing the rapidly changing lifestyles and newfound freedom of the 1910s and 20s. She dedicated her entire life to making women look and feel beautiful, and would often say, "When a woman smiles, then her dress should smile, too." Remembered as one of the most innovative and intellectual of all haute couturieres, she is perhaps best known for visualizing fabric in an entirely different way. Her pioneering technique of cutting diagonally across the grain, on the bias instead of the typical straight cuts, yielded a graceful fluidity. Vionnet did not draw her designs, but draped fabrics on a 33-inch wooden mannequin, enabling her to design in the round. She would then give the precisely draped material to her patternmaker to expertly render.

Vionnet's dresses did not allow for more traditional side seams, so her spiral seams followed the contours of the body to create an alluring silhouette. She had yardage woven to her specifications, at more than 78 inches wide, so her garments could move with ease. Her clients scandalously wore little or no lingerie beneath their gowns, enabling more freedom of movement. Vionnet's bias cut gowns were extremely popular and could be seen on international stars of the day, including Katharine Hepburn, Joan Crawford, Greta Garbo, and Marlene Dietrich.

Sadly, when World War II broke out, she closed her business and never opened it again. But Vionnet's legacy lives on as her bias cut remains a strong influence on contemporary fashion and has been seen in the collections of Halston, Azzedine Alaïa, Issey Miyake, and countless others.

PAUL POIRET

1879 – 1944

PARIS (FRANCE)

PAUL POIRET

The modernist designer who freed women from the corset

Modernist Paul Poiret was a visionary and an open-minded couturier with a design sense well ahead of his time. His unbound imagination intuitively embraced the future as he challenged fundamental assumptions about how women should dress.

The son of a cloth merchant, Poiret apprenticed with an umbrella maker. He would gather fabric scraps from the floor, draping them onto a wooden doll for his own experiments. Years later, he would be the first to drape fabric directly on live models as opposed to cutting from precise paper patterns.

Poiret changed not only the direction of costume history, but also guided it toward modern design with his technical and marketing acumen. He was the first couturier to introduce a signature fragrance and the first to combine fashion with interior design—today's "branded lifestyle"—with coordinated fabrics, wall paintings, and cushions for the home.

In 1903, Poiret opened his own maison de couture in Paris. Instead of the tight-fitting petticoats and corsets that were popular at the time, Poiret's designs were meant to be worn by an un-corseted, slim figure. Inspired by the impresario Sergei Diaghilev and the shocking colors and transparent fabrics of the Ballets Russes costumes, Poiret's collections featured romantic, exotic clothing. Vividly colored gowns and mysterious silhouettes echoed his fantasies about the exotic East: the "lampshade" tunic, the turban, the kimono coat, the empire waist, and the "harem" pantaloons.

But by the time he enlisted in the French army during World War I, fashion's focus was shifting to utility, function and rationality, not the elaborately embellished Poiret gowns. Unable to accept this new direction toward simplicity, he persisted through the 1920s, eventually closing his house of couture in 1929.

His 1931 autobiography, *King of Fashion*, remains an important fashion history reference to this day. Yet by the end of his life, he was all but forgotten. He died penniless in Paris in 1944.

COCO CHANEL

The queen of luxury

While the name Chanel is now associated with luxury, it was not always the case for Gabrielle "Coco" Chanel. Born in a charity hospital in Saumur, France, Chanel grew up in poverty. After her mother died, she was sent to live in an orphanage. It was there that the nuns taught her to sew, providing her with a skill that would serve her well in life. In later life, she would retell the story of her childhood differently, including glamorous accounts which were often untrue.

As a young woman, Chanel lived as the mistress to several gentlemen who supported her career as a milliner and a dressmaker. Famously, she began her career using remainders of military cotton jersey, developing casual dress worn for leisure and sport in the color beige, her renowned color. "Luxury must be comfortable, or it is not luxury." She is known for her "little black dress," an innovation in cut and proportion worn for either day or evening.

A creative designer, Chanel extended influence beyond couture by designing jewelry, handbags, shoes, and fragrance, including her signature scent, Chanel No. 5, as well as her famous intermeshed CC logo. Chanel's fabric choices were elegant: lace, tulle, embroidery, and delicate silks. She gave attention to detail, creating couture for the self-assured, chic woman.

Chanel closed her house in 1939, ostracized for her relationship with a German diplomat. In 1954, she returned to Paris, introducing the "Chanel" suit: a three-piece designed to assure comfort and ease of movement. It was loosely woven with a collarless, braid-trimmed cropped jacket and skirt. Unusually, the jacket had pockets and lapels edged in braid. The style remains popular to this day.

Chanel continued designing until her death in 1971 at the age of 87. Her legacy remains and she was the only fashion designer included on *Time* magazine's list of the 100 most influential people of the 20th century.

COCO CHANEL

1883 – 1971

SAUMUR (FRANCE)

ELSA SCHIAPARELLI

1890 – 1973

ROME (ITALY)

ELSA SCHIAPARELLI

The provocateur who shocked the world with her visionary designs

Elsa Schiaparelli was born into an aristocratic family in Rome. She spent her young adult years looking for adventure, living in London, New York, and Boston, before settling in Paris in 1922. Schiaparelli had no formal training in patternmaking or clothing construction, coming to fashion as a career in her 30s. Despite being financially supported by her wealthy family, after being deserted by her husband, Schiaparelli wanted to earn an independent income to support herself and her daughter. Under the influence of her mentor, Paul Poiret, Schiaparelli began making her own clothes. She relied on her own creativity as well as inspiration from Surrealist artists including Jean Cocteau, Salvador Dali, and Man Ray.

Schiaparelli created knitwear featuring optical illusions, incorporating a bow or a scarf around the neck knitted into a sweater's design. In 1927, she established her maison de couture in Paris where she designed haute couture until the 1950s. Schiaparelli was the archetype of modernity and quite the provocateur. In 1947, her interpretation of bright pink was "shocking" and became the rage in the world of fashion. She was witty in her design of textiles, jewelry, perfume, lingerie, ski wear, swimsuits, and even eyewear. Schiaparelli created textiles patterned with a lobster, tree bark, newspaper clippings, and two people kissing. A compact powder case appeared to be a rotary telephone. A pair of gloves mimicked a skunk crawling up the arm. Miniature acrobats, vegetables, mirrors, and insects functioned as buttons.

Her fashion silhouettes were visionary, with her revolutionary design for the wraparound day dress, an evening dress with a bustle, or a cape with feathers. She was the first to use camouflage pattern in fashion, she invented the divided skirt, and made the zipper intentionally visible as a design element.

Despite her success, Schiaparelli closed her business in 1951 as Christian Dior's "New Look" became the popular fashion of the day. She lived a comfortable retirement and died in 1973 at the age of 83.

CRISTÓBAL BALENCIAGA

1895 – 1972

GETARIA (SPAIN)

CRISTÓBAL BALENCIAGA

The original design king

Many fashion designers referred to the Spanish couturier Cristóbal Balenciaga as "master of us all"—quite a sign of respect from his peers. Balenciaga grew up in Getaria, Spain, the son of a fisherman father and a seamstress mother. He would sit with his mother as she worked and eventually went on to apprentice for a tailor. A wealthy Marchioness took note of his innate talent and hired him to design for her. Believing in the budding designer's creativity, she sent a teenaged Balenciaga to Madrid to learn the trade so he would be expertly proficient in realizing his sketches, patternmaking, and cutting.

Balenciaga successfully opened his first boutique in San Sebastian, followed by two more, in Barcelona and Madrid. But during the Spanish Civil War, he closed his shops and fled to Paris, where he established his maison de haute couture in 1937.

In 1951, among other haute couture designers, Balenciaga was praised as the designer with the most original silhouettes and structures. He was an expert at proportion and measurement when interpreting the natural form. In the mid-1950s he designed loose, comfortable garments eliminating the waist and extending the shoulders. His tunic, chemise, and babydoll designs were at the height of inventive fashion. Later, he realized his interpretations of the empire waist and the Japanese kimono. He designed garments with volume and an ingenious coat with one seam.

Disappointed by the lack of skill and innovation in couture in the late 1960s, Balenciaga closed his maison and retired to Spain, claiming that "high fashion is mortally wounded." Upon his death in 1972, *Women's Wear Daily* reported that "The King is Dead." But Balenciaga's legacy lives on and in 2011, the Balenciaga Museum was inaugurated in his hometown of Getaria.

ANN LOWE

The designer who broke barriers

Ann Lowe's fashions were popular from the 1920s into the 1960s. As an African American at that time, this was no small feat, considering that her work was favored among American upper class families including the Du Ponts, Rockefellers, and Posts. She even designed Jacqueline Kennedy's ivory silk taffeta wedding dress in 1953, but was not credited for it until after President Kennedy's death in 1963.

Born in rural Alabama, Lowe's interest in fashion design, dressmaking, and sewing came from her mother and grandmother, seamstresses who owned a shop frequented by Montgomery's elite. After marriage and motherhood, Lowe and her son moved to Harlem in 1917 so she could hone her talent at design school. While difficult to imagine now, Lowe was required to study in a separate room due to the color of her skin. After graduating in 1919, she opened a salon in Tampa, Florida, creating fashions for the wealthy white community.

She returned to New York City in 1928 and continued designing for high society through commissions from Henri Bendel, Neiman Marcus, and Saks Fifth Avenue. Olivia de Havilland wore an Ann Lowe creation when she accepted her Academy Award in 1946, although Lowe was not credited for her work. In 1950, she established Ann Lowe's Gowns, guaranteeing credit for her creations. The press noted that she incorporated luxurious materials, expert handwork and perfect stitching techniques. *Ebony* magazine referred to her as "The Dean of American Designers."

Lowe was obliged to declare bankruptcy in 1962 as her expenses mounted, including the high salaries she paid her workroom staff. She often was unable to make a profit, as her wealthy clients would talk her out of charging what her creations were worth. She opened Ann Lowe Originals on Madison Avenue in 1968, thanks to the generosity of an anonymous friend who paid off her debts. After suffering from years of eye-related illnesses, Lowe retired in 1972 and died in Queens, New York, in 1981 at the age of 82.

ANN LOWE

1898 – 1981

CLAYTON, ALABAMA (USA)

CHRISTIAN DIOR

1905 – 1957

GRANVILLE (FRANCE)

CHRISTIAN DIOR

The creator of the New Look

Post World War II restrictions, the legendary couturier Christian Dior fine-tuned his creativity by responding to the desires of women who required glamorous gowns and luxurious daywear. As far as Dior was concerned, there was nothing trivial about haute couture, famously noting, "The world has changed its pace and fashion has changed with it, therefore novelty is the essence of the fashion trade."

Born to a wealthy French family, Dior studied political science and his parents hoped he would one day become a diplomat. Dior's artistic sensibility won out, and he instead owned an art gallery representing some of the noted artists of the day, including Pablo Picasso. When his family's finances diminished, he made ends meet by selling fashion sketches.

Backed by cotton entrepreneur Marcel Boussac, he opened his House of Dior in 1946. The fashion press enthusiastically wrote about his inaugural collection in 1947 and every collection that followed, providing his spectators with new silhouettes from his Paris atelier every six months.

Dior's single, most important design was the ensemble labeled "The Bar." It featured a radical design: the jacket sloped at the shoulders, closely fit at the corseted waist, and was padded below the hips, further suggesting femininity. The full and pleated skirt was worn to the ankle. This look came to be known as the "New Look." A rebuttal to the drab clothing of wartime, each dress used 20 yards of fabric, supporting Dior's wish for very full, pleated, sculpted and gathered garments. His fashions were so well structured that no lingerie was needed.

Dior's extraordinarily successful career in design and business was brief, ending with his death from a heart attack while at a health spa in Italy. He was only 52. According to Dior's wishes, his 21-year-old assistant, Yves Saint Laurent, became the artistic director of the House of Dior.

PIERRE CARDIN

The visionary designer known for his futuristic designs

Born in Italy, Pierre Cardin fled to France as a young child with his parents and nine siblings to escape post-World War I fascism in the country. From his childhood, Cardin was interested in dressmaking. He was fond of ballet and theater and dreamed of an acting career. While attending performances, he was fascinated with beautiful costumes and stage sets.

Although he moved to Paris to study architecture, Cardin worked with haute couture designers Jean Paquin and Elsa Schiaparelli, then couturier Christian Dior. At the House of Paquin, he realized his dream of working in the theater, helping design the costumes for *Beauty and the Beast*, collaborating with artists Jean Cocteau and Christian Berard to create masks for the film.

Cardin established his atelier, presenting his first collection in 1953. He opened Eve, then Adam, his first boutiques in Paris. Cardin was a visionary, and in the 1950s and 60s was recognized for his bold cosmic and futuristic fashions. His sharply delineated short vinyl tunics and use of vinyl accessories, including brooches fashioned from carpenter's nails, helmets, and plexiglass visors, launched what became known as the Space Age look. As early as 1957, the fiercely independent Cardin introduced ready-to-wear designs for both men and women, beginning a revolution in the production of designer fashions.

He was endlessly curious, experimenting with abstraction, exaggeration, techniques, and technology. In 1968, Cardin created the sculptural Egg Carton dress made with dynel, an early high-tech material that when heat-treated, was molded to feature three-dimensional geometric designs.

Recognizing the value of his brand, Cardin extended his name to cosmetics and perfume, and, to the horror of other haute couturiers, began licensing his name as a brand associated with various everyday accessories. It was a lucrative move, followed by his foray into industrial design, textiles for automobile interiors, and plexiglass "utilitarian sculptures" that served as furniture.

PIERRE CARDIN

1922 – 2020

TREVISO (ITALY)

HUBERT DE GIVENCHY

1927 – 2018

BEAUVAIS (FRANCE)

HUBERT DE GIVENCHY

The creator of personality

Hubert de Givenchy came from a noble and artistic-leaning family. After his father died from influenza when Givenchy was only three years old, he was raised by his mother and maternal grandmother, an artist who was the owner and director of the historic Gobelins Manufactory and Beauvais tapestry factories. His great-grandfather was a set designer who also created designs for the Beauvais factory, including a set of 13 designs for the Elysée Palace. One of his great-great-grandfathers designed sets for the Paris Opera.

At the age of 17, Givenchy left his aristocratic family's estate in Beauvais, France, to begin his studies at Paris's École des Beaux-Arts, before going on to study law. Yet, he was drawn to fashion design while working as an apprentice to the couturier Jacques Fath. He later worked in the ateliers of Robert Piguet, Lucien LeLong, and Elsa Schiaparelli.

Known for simple glamour, Givenchy's first collection featured flawless craftsmanship in exquisite separates, elegant coats, and jewel-like ball gowns. He was the first among haute couture designers to create luxury ready-to-wear. His collections included innovative accessories, silk prints and embroidered fabrics. Both he and his idol, Cristóbal Balenciaga, were passionate about linear looks, which inspired Givenchy to introduce the "sack" silhouette which would prove to be iconic.

Givenchy designed for many celebrity clients, including Audrey Hepburn. She was his muse, and he defined her cinematic style in the films *Charade*, *Love in the Afternoon* and *Funny Girl*, among others. In the 1961 classic *Breakfast at Tiffany's*, one of the best-known scenes sees Hepburn stepping out of a taxi clad in a sleeveless little black dress that he designed. According to Hepburn, "He is more than a couturier; he is a creator of personality." As business partners and friends, they were a memorable couple in the fashion press for years. He was a towering 6'6" to her diminutive stature. In his later years, Givenchy lived at his country estate near Paris where he died in his sleep at the age of 91.

SONIA RYKIEL

1930 – 2016

NEUILLY-SUR-SEINE (FRANCE)

SONIA RYKIEL

The queen of knits

Women's Wear Daily rightfully called French prêt-à-porter designer Sonia Rykiel the "Queen of Knits." The eldest of five sisters, Rykiel was born to Jewish parents in Neuilly-sur-Seine, France. At the age of 17, she was already harnessing her design talents as the window dresser of a Parisian textile shop. Five years later, she married Sam Rykiel, the owner of an elegant boutique in Paris.

Unsatisfied with apparel for expectant mothers, she stitched a knit dress and sweater for herself that clung to the body. It was a sharp departure from what had been available and would become known as the Poor Boy Sweater. The iconic ribbed skin-tight look was featured on the cover of *Elle* magazine in 1963 and became a favorite of Audrey Hepburn, Catherine Deneuve, Brigitte Bardot, Twiggy, and many others, helping to define the look of the swinging 1960s.

Rykiel opened her own luxury boutique in 1968. She pioneered new variations on contemporary fashion: slogans knitted into her garments, seams on the outside of apparel, and hems left unfinished. Credited with helping to popularize wearing the color black, Rykiel famously noted, "It's not true that clothes look better on skinny girls—what counts is the attitude." Rykiel wore clothes from her own label and preferred to dress simply, generally in dark green, brown, navy blue, and black. She was well known for her signature hairstyle—a bright orange frizzled bob.

Rykiel's career expanded to include menswear, children's clothing, accessories, cosmetics, fragrances, and interiors. She was also a published author of several books on fashion, a collection of stories for children, a novel, and magazine columns. Sadly, Rykiel suffered from Parkinson's disease for nearly two decades, eventually dying from complications of the disease in 2016.

HALSTON

The hatmaker who revolutionized 1970s fashion

Roy Halston Frowick was known as Halston since childhood. By the 1970s, the handsome, soft spoken, and lanky American fashion designer would become an international creative and social sensation. He was among the first to design genderless fashions and to feature models of various races. A minimalist, he constructed sexy elegant garments in luxurious fabrics and introduced washable Ultrasuede. His aesthetic redefined the casualwear worn by American women, from urban streets to the dance floor at the notorious New York City club Studio 54.

Growing up in Evansville, Indiana, Halston came to Chicago in 1952 where he attended evening classes as the School of the Art Institute and worked as a window dresser. In 1953, he opened his own hat business. Many of his clients were celebrities who attracted the fashion press. Halston's fame grew when he created the iconic pillbox hat that Jacqueline Kennedy wore at President John F. Kennedy's inauguration in 1961.

When hats were no longer fashionable, Halston turned to fashion design, opening his first boutique in New York and launching his first ready-to-wear line that popularized shirtwaist dresses, caftans, and matte jersey halter-top dresses. His posse of models, the Halstonettes, not only walked the runways, but brought glamour to the dance floor. His clients included Liza Minelli, Elizabeth Taylor, Bianca Jagger, and Diana Vreeland, among other stars.

"There are no problems, only opportunities," he said. Halston reshaped the business of fashion when he licensed his name to J.C. Penney and designed uniforms for Braniff Airlines—both revolutionary at the time. Throughout the 1970s, he expanded his label to include menswear, luggage, handbags, lingerie, linens, and a signature fragrance, "Halston."

Declining health and poor business planning eventually lost him the right to design for his own label. Halston died in 1990 from AIDS-related complications.

HALSTON

1932 – 1990

DES MOINES, IOWA (USA)

VALENTINO GARAVANI

Born 1932

VOGHERA (ITALY)

VALENTINO GARAVANI

The Italian king of glamour

Known as Valentino throughout his glamorous career, Valentino Garavani is a haute-couture and ready-to-wear designer known for his signature color, "rosso Valentino." Growing up in Voghera, Italy, he was interested in dressmaking and art. Valentino studied in Paris, refining his talent at the École des Beaux-Arts and the Chambre Syndicale de la Couture Parisienne. Following his rigorous training, he worked for Jacques Fath and Cristóbal Balenciaga, among other couture designers.

At the age of 27, Valentino returned to Italy to work for several prestigious Roman couturiers. With financial support from his father, he opened his fashion house in 1960. Later that year, he met Giancarlo Giammetti, which proved to be a significant moment as they would become lifelong business and life partners.

In 1962, Valentino enjoyed a spectacular reception when he introduced his first collection in Florence. Guests enthusiastically embraced his elegant ballgowns, pencil-thin skirts, and sculpted dresses with voluminous shoulders. He famously noted, "Elegance is the balance between proportion, emotion and surprise."

In the mid-1960s, he opened a ready-to-wear boutique on Rome's Via Gregoriana, a destination of the wealthy, celebrities, and aristocrats. Jacqueline Kennedy was both a couture client and a friend. Valentino's fashion shows became sought-after social events offering glamour beyond anything seen before. Valentino was known for impeccable tailoring, and in the 1970s, he emphasized skirts, fitted knee-high boots with mini-skirts and hot pants, trousers, and ethnic looks with fit-and-flare silhouettes. He designed costumes for the ballet and opera and introduced a line of fragrances in 1978. Valentino and Giammetti maintained control over the Valentino brand, which supported their extravagant lifestyle.

After announcing his retirement in 2007, several exhibitions in Paris and London showcased Valentino's work, together with a virtual museum experience and later, several documentary films. The Valentino brand persists to this day, with ready-to-wear and couture created by a succession of notable designers.

KARL LAGERFELD

1933 – 2019

HAMBURG (GERMANY)

KARL LAGERFELD

The fashion visionary with lasting influence

Born in Hamburg, Germany, Karl Lagerfeld was interested in the arts from a young age. As a child, he continually sketched in class regardless of what other students were doing. A frequent visitor to the Hamburger Kunsthalle museum, Lagerfeld later said he learned more from those museum visits than he ever did in school.

After winning an award in a coat design competition in 1954, Lagerfeld was hired by Pierre Cardin, then by Pierre Balmain. He went on to design freelance for numerous brands, including Charles Jourdan, Chloé, Krizia, and Valentino.

Lagerfeld contributed to the new fashions of the mid-1970s that excluded linings, padding, and even hemming from voluminous, thin-fabric garments that allowed for a comfortable, layered style. In Paris, he was easily spotted on the streets by his signature powdered white hair worn in a ponytail, black sunglasses, fingerless gloves, and high, starched collars. Despite his public appearance to the contrary, he was funny, warm, and sensitive. On the runway, he believed he was a performer.

From 1983 until his death, Lagerfeld held the position of designer for the modern revival of the house of Chanel. An avid photographer, he photographed many of Chanel's promotional materials. He established his eponymous label in 1984. As consultant director, he modernized furs in design for the Italian house of Fendi. His boundary-pushing collaborations with brands like H&M, Macy's, and Coca-Cola were ahead of their time.

The multi-talented Lagerfeld also created illustrations for Hans Christian Andersen's *The Emperor's New Clothes* and created costumes for Milan's Teatro alla Scala, the Florence opera house, and the Ballet de Monte Carlo. Although he insisted that no one ever know the date of his birth, school records confirm that he was born in 1933, thus making him 85 years old at his death in 2019.

GIORGIO ARMANI

The innovator of androgenous style

Giorgio Armani was born in Piacenza, Italy. He initially aspired to be a doctor, but after studying medicine for three years at the University of Milan, Armani left school to join the army. After leaving the army, in 1957, he got his start working as a window display designer, then sales clerk and buyer in the menswear department for the Milan department store La Rinascente. After seven years, he began training for his career in fashion in the workrooms of Nino Cerruti, starting with menswear. Concurrently, he also freelanced, contributing designs to many manufacturers.

In 1975, supported by his business partner, Sergio Galeotti, he opened a design studio in Milan. That year, he presented his first collection of men's and women's ready-to-wear under his own name, staged at his 17th-century palazzo in Milan. The following year, he established his eponymous label of ready-to-wear for men and women featuring what would become his signature androgynous style. Armani has said, "I was the first to soften the image of men, and harden the image of women. I dressed men in women's fabrics, and adapted menswear to what women wanted and needed—the power suit."

Armani's work lies at the nexus of fashion and art. In 2000, the Guggenheim Museum in New York exhibited Armani's work, a first for a living designer. He creates timeless styles in luxurious fabrics for fluid, relaxed apparel, and exquisitely embroidered evening gowns worn with ease for streamlined modernity.

A savvy businessman, Armani has diversified his brand, embracing the designer lifestyle by introducing perfume, accessories, jeans, sportswear, underwear, swimwear, the lower-priced Emporio Armani line, and a limited-edition collection of couture dresses. Further broadening his namesake label, he branched out to create Armani hotels, interior furnishings, and music.

In 2002, his Armani Privé spring/summer fashion show was streamed on the MSN Web portal and Cingular cellular phones, making him the first designer to broadcast a haute couture fashion show live on the Internet.

GIORGIO ARMANI

Born 1934

PIACENZA (ITALY)

AZZEDINE ALAÏA

1935 – 2017

TUNIS (TUNISIA)

AZZEDINE ALAÏA

The designer who embraced second-skin dressing

Diminutive in stature, Tunisian-born Azzedine Alaïa was an uncompromising visionary in the world of fashion. He studied at the Tunis Institute of Fine Arts, where he gained an awareness of the human form when he began studying sculpture. For his own education, he would disassemble vintage couture garments and then reassemble them to study how they were made.

In 1957, he moved to Paris to work for Christian Dior, Guy Laroche, and Thierry Mugler before he opened his own small atelier. He maintained his salon for more than 20 years, dressing members of the elite and celebrities. Alaïa was admired for his autonomy, a willingness to not compromise, and a respect for discerning luxury: "I have always wanted women to be free. I hope my dresses give them that lightness. The greatest compliment is when they look at themselves and say to me: 'I feel free.'"

Alaïa dedicated his life to believing that fashion was more than garments, it was an element in the self determination of women. Thus, his fashions were timeless. His designs were known for a slim fit and expert tailoring, emphasizing seaming, leather work, and inventive knits. His trademark was second-skin dressing. His color palette was somber, black, neutral and earthy, and his silhouettes were voluptuous. Alaïa's seductive, clinging clothes also were a success in New York, where the fashion press dubbed him "The King of Cling."

In a larger Parisian atelier on rue du Parc-Royal, Alaïa produced his first ready-to-wear collection in 1980. Instead of conforming to the standard fashion week shows that happened twice a year, Alaïa instead invited guests to see his small collection at his salon for a quiet and elegant showing.

At home, Alaïa would dress in a collarless Chinese-style shirt and pants for intimate lunch and dinner gatherings where he cooked for his guests and regaled them with stories. Beloved by many in the fashion world, Alaïa died in Paris at the age of 82.

YVES SAINT LAURENT

1936 – 2008

ORAN (ALGERIA)

YVES SAINT LAURENT

The designer who embraced gender fluidity and a diverse runway

Born to wealthy parents, Yves Saint Laurent grew up in a villa on the Mediterranean Sea in Oran, Algeria. As a child, he was bullied in school and found comfort in making detailed paper dolls for his sisters, and as a teen, making dresses for his sisters and mother. During a trip to Paris in 1952, he met an editor for *French Vogue* who encouraged his talent and later introduced him to Christian Dior. A year later, Saint Laurent moved to Paris to study at the Chambre Syndicale de la Haute Couture. He became Dior's protégé, where he refined his innate talent, and was named head designer at the House of Dior at the age of 21, following Dior's untimely death in 1957.

In 1960, he was conscripted into military service during the French-Algerian War, but after three weeks was hospitalized due to the stress caused by humiliation from homophobic soldiers. After being fired from Dior during his hospitalization, he sued for breach of contract and won, helping Saint Laurent establish his namesake haute couture label.

Reflecting the pop culture movement, Saint Laurent's legendary "Le Smoking" black tuxedo foreshadowed gender fluidity in fashion. He introduced thigh-high boots and the pea coat for women, sheer blouses, jumpsuits, the safari jacket and the beatnik look. In 1965, he paid tribute to Dutch artist Piet Mondrian by designing a collection of dresses that referenced the painter's iconic abstract works. They had a modern feel and were incredibly well received.

Even though his signature YSL logo has gone mainstream, it still evokes luxury. He was the first Parisian couturier to feature Black and Asian models on the runway, embrace gender fluidity, and to integrate non-European cultural references in his collections. Saint Laurent was the first living designer to be featured in an exhibit at New York's Metropolitan Museum of Art, in 1983. In 2002, Saint Laurent retired, and died in Paris in 2008.

ISSEY MIYAKE

The designer who made origami fashions

The visionary designer Miyake Kazunaru, known as Issey Miyake, survived the atomic bomb that devasted Hiroshima at the end of World War II. As a child, he dreamed of being a dancer and an artist, although he took an interest in the photographs in his sister's fashion magazines. After completing his studies in graphic design, Miyake went to Paris to study tailoring and dressmaking. He apprenticed with designers Guy Laroche and Hubert de Givenchy, then with American icon Geoffrey Beene in New York.

In 1970, he returned to Tokyo to open Miyake Design Studio and launch his initial unique layering system. Miyake's creations of origami-folded fabric made his work instantly recognizable and internationally admired. For his 1989 pleated collection, Miyake created a radical cubist vision of the human body in movement. He experimented with natural and synthetic fibers, including traditional Japanese oil-soaked paper, monofilament, and molded silicone. Miyake created geometric shapes and bias draping to accommodate motion, relying on the body to bring his designs to life. He combined Eastern and Western sensibilities, exploring the nature, form, and function of apparel.

His ready to wear Pleats Please line allowed for the body to move freely, while enabling the fabric to maintain its shape. Single pieces of polyester fabric, when cut and sewn flat, were far larger than the finished pleated garments. The completed piece was then pressed into multiple tiny pleats between two sheets of paper, creating permanent pleats, magically transforming the original cut pieces.

Miyake's A-POC ("A Piece of Cloth") was made from a single thread guided by industrial knitting machines. The garment was essentially a long tube of jersey. It was the intrepid client who clipped and shaped the garment, but only once. Miyake's work has been honored by many. In 1998, an exhibit in Paris presented a 30-year retrospective of Miyake's fashions and collaborations with artists, dancers, and photographers, along with an exploration of his experimentations with textiles and technology.

ISSEY MIYAKE

1938 – 2022

HIROSHIMA (JAPAN)

VIVIENNE WESTWOOD

The designer who made punk and new wave fashions mainstream

Considered to be among the most provocative fashion designers, Vivienne Westwood was also a passionate humanitarian and environmental activist. A self-taught designer, Westwood got her start selling her hand-made jewelry at London's Portobello Road market. Her intuitive creativity would eventually distinguish her as a world-renowned fashion designer.

In 1965, she met Malcom McLaren, who would become her husband and business partner. McLaren later became manager of the punk band the Sex Pistols, which helped Westwood gain attention as the band wore her designs—ripped t-shirts with anti-establishment slogans and clothing inspired by the S&M culture. Together, Westwood and McLaren synthesized hard-core fashion and music, epitomizing the punk scene. To their delight, they riled up the right-wing press with their outrageous and naughty imagery.

Westwood and McLaren's raucous first runway collection featured men and women dressed as pirates in frilly shirts with puffy sleeves, cementing Westwood's independence as a designer who succeeded at integrating the look and feel of the punk scene and new-wave fashions into the mainstream.

In disagreement over partnership, McLaren left to find fortune in Los Angeles as a movie producer and their relationship ended in divorce. For years, Westwood created collections inspired by 18th and 19th century sources, including Jean-Honoré Fragonard, François Boucher, and Thomas Gainsborough, and by historic dress, including the 19th-century bustle. Her infamous adaption was the mini-crini, an abbreviated version of the Victorian crinoline, which debuted in 1985.

Westwood was twice named British Designer of the Year and was appointed an Officer of the Order of the British Empire for services to fashion design. In 2004, a retrospective at London's Victoria & Albert Museum celebrated her 34 years in fashion. Following her death in 2022, her husband and design partner Andreas Kronthaler continues to design for her label.

VIVIENNE WESTWOOD

1941 – 2022

TINTWISTLE, ENGLAND (UK)

REI KAWAKUBO

The visionary designer who continues to redefine fashion

A true disruptor, many think of Rei Kawakubo as the fashion iconoclast of the 21st century. The daughter of a strong-willed mother, she studied fine arts and literature at Tokyo's Keio University. Kawakubo never studied fashion, sewing, cutting, or draping, but got her start in the fashion industry working as a stylist. In 1969, Kawakubo began designing and making her own clothes under the label Comme des Garçons, which means "like boys" in French.

Kawakubo's collections have been described as antifashion. They challenge traditional concepts of beauty, shocking the critics with their anarchic punk spirit. The 1982 "Destroy" collection featured oversized knit sweaters with holes that she called lace. The press dubbed her dark, deconstructed style "Hiroshima chic." Her sculptural garments were primarily black, oversized and asymmetrical, twisted, and bulged, not conforming to the body. Kawakubo says that she designs in three colors of black to dress her followers, known as the "crows."

In 2005, Kawakubo told *The New Yorker* that she "never intended to start a revolution," that she only intended to show "what I thought was strong and beautiful."

Kawakubo's designs can be so abstract that they are virtually unwearable. Her 1997 collection, "Dress Meets Body, Body Meets," featuring lumps of padding positioned in unflattering places, was roundly criticized for disfiguring the woman's form. Yet that collection inspired dancers' garments for *Scenario*, a dance performance choreographed by Merce Cunningham, the same year.

Although her work has not received the positive reaction from the press as some of her peers, Kawakubo is supported and admired within the fashion industry and the arts community. In 2017, the Metropolitan Museum of Art presented the exhibit *Rei Kawakubo/Commes des Garçons, Art of the In-Between*, the first time a designer was given a solo show at the museum in 34 years. Today, Kawakubo continues at the helm of Comme des Garçons as creative director.

REI KAWAKUBO

Born 1942

TOKYO (JAPAN)

STEPHEN BURROWS

Born 1943

NEWARK, NEW JERSEY (USA)

STEPHEN BURROWS

The disco designer

As a child, Stephen Burrows was fascinated by the zigzag stitch made on his grandmother's sewing machine. It would become his signature red trademark top stitch. In high school, Burrows loved to dance the mambo and created dresses for his dance partners in wild color combinations, also becoming one of his trademarks.

Burrows began school at the Philadelphia Museum College of Art with the intention of being an art teacher before transferring to New York's Fashion Institute of Technology. As a student, Burrows began working with knits and matte jersey, producing clothes for "going out."

The nightlife of 1960s New York City fueled his imagination and designs. He co-founded the "O" boutique in New York and later managed his own boutique at Henri Bendel before establishing his own label. In 1973, Burrows was the youngest of five American designers to show at the famous Battle at Versailles Fashion Show, a runway extravaganza, to raise money for the restoration of the Palace of Versailles.

One of the first African American designers to achieve international acclaim, Burrows established a mainstream, high-fashion clientele. A champion of the disco style, his designs were celebrated for their graphic color blocking and use of matte jersey fabric. His clothing moved with the body, hugging the wearer, including metallic mesh in slinky silhouettes. His clothing was cut and sewn in 45-degree angles and pieced together, deconstructed, all with expert tailoring. His signature hem has a wavy edge he calls the "lettuce hem."

Celebrities including Barbra Streisand, Cher, The Supremes, Bette Midler, and Michelle Obama have worn his clothing, and his work has been honored by the CFDA. Today, Burrows's fashions are still vibrant, bold, exciting, and energetic, with rainbows of daring color combinations that shout, "get up and move."

YOHJI YAMAMOTO

Born 1943

TOKYO (JAPAN)

YOHJI YAMAMOTO

The master of tailoring

Although he graduated with a degree in law, Yohji Yamamoto soon realized that a legal career was not for him. Yamamoto's mother was a dressmaker, and after graduation, he worked in his mother's shop to learn from her sewing assistants. At her request, he attended Bunka Fashion College. During his time in school, he developed his theories in fashion.

In 1977, Yamamoto introduced his first collection, Y's, in Tokyo. He bewildered the audience with unfinished, worn, and erratically constructed garments. Since then, he constantly explores the relationship between the feminine and masculine, creating clothes for women with an intellectual emphasis. Importantly, he believes that he is "an epicurean. I am an anarchist, I hate power."

Yamamoto is known for his futuristic sense of design as well as his references to dress of Europe in the 19th century. His signature silhouettes are often oversized, draping and irregular at hems. Yamamoto is a master of tailoring, creating avant-garde silhouettes, predominantly in the color black, suggesting both submission and transgression. "Black is modest, and arrogant at the same time."

In 1981, he introduced a prêt-à-porter collection in Paris, and since then, has expanded his genius to ballet and opera costume. Famously, he has created costume and streetwear for the late dancer Pina Bausch and his friend Elton John. During runway shows, you can often hear Yamamoto's voice singing.

In addition to his Yohji Yamamoto and Y's lines, he also has several other lines, including Costume d'Homme, Pour Homme, and the diffusion line Coming Soon. He has also collaborated with a number of brands, including Hermès, Adidas, and Mikimoto.

Yamamoto's work has achieved a global following and he has been the recipient of numerous accolades, including Japan's Medal of Honor and the French Legion of Honor for his contributions to the arts.

GIANNI VERSACE

1944 – 1997

REGGIO CALABRIA (ITALY)

DONATELLA VERSACE

Born 1955

REGGIO CALABRIA (ITALY)

GIANNI & DONATELLA VERSACE

The designer who connected fashion and music

Gianni Versace is remembered as a legendary fashion designer of the 1980s and 90s. He designed ready-to-wear for royalty and celebrities and is known for his risk-taking fashions and glamorous lifestyle. Tragically, his life was cut short when he was murdered in 1997 at his home in Miami, Florida.

Versace arrived in Milan in 1972 after working in Reggio Calabria with his mother, a dressmaker. He worked as a design assistant for several Milanese design houses and then established his label Gianni Versace in 1978. He created voluptuous ensembles, including his iconic, sophisticated bondage dresses, though detractors considered these fashions vulgar. At the end of his 25-year career, he was at "the top," moderating his sensational earlier work to create refined and colorful fashions.

Seasonal runway collections were staged as rock concerts at his palatial headquarters. He is thought of as the instigator of the fashion industry's high-powered, celebrity-infatuated industry. The name "supermodel" was given to his highly paid models, including Linda Evangelista, Naomi Campbell, and Cindy Crawford.

In 1989, he introduced his first line of couture and created costumes for the opera and ballet. Versace explored costume design as another interest throughout his career. His company has expanded to produce clothing for men, as well as handbags, jewelry, perfume, and home furnishings.

Since his death, his sister Donatella Versace has been the creative director for the label. Her brother had always valued her intuition and critique at the beginning of his career. His perfume, Blonde, was created in her honor. She has proceeded with the company's image through her savvy public relations abilities and positive design direction, leading the company through a design reinvention. Gianni's work was honored by a posthumous retrospective at the Costume Institute of the Metropolitan Museum of Art that ran from 1997-98.

MIUCCIA PRADA

The designer of understated elegance

Italian designer Miuccia Prada was born into a family of fashion. Her grandfather founded the Prada brand in 1913 as a producer of renowned leather suitcases, handbags, and steamer trunks. The company was later run by Miuccia's mother. The venerable Italian brand reflects the taste of confident, intellectual men and women.

Prada was educated at the University of Milan and received a PhD in political science which led to her feminist activism in left-wing politics. In 1970, she started managing the family business. Prada worked with her future husband, Patrizio Bertelli, to reenvision the Prada brand and introduce a modern image. Their professional relationship eventually turned personal, and they married in 1987.

In the 1980s, the company expanded internationally, opening additional stores and introducing a shoe line. Gaining an enthusiastic following, in 1988, Prada launched her first ready-to-wear collection, featuring exquisitely constructed nylon parkas that are durable yet stylish. One of her pivotal innovations was a line of unlabeled handbags constructed from nylon. Prada introduced Miu Miu, its more youthful line, in 1992. With Bertelli at the helm as business manager, the Prada brand has expanded to include a menswear line.

As a minimalist, Prada embraces a traditional style, balancing understated glamour with refined elegance at a time when the flagrant sex appeal of many competitors prompts a reevaluation of femininity. Her clean and simple silhouettes in muted, basic colors are exquisitely tailored in luxurious fabrics.

Prada's approach to design extends to architecture as well. She commissioned architect Rem Koolhaas to create Prada's pathbreaking "Epicenter" boutique in New York; the "Epicenter" store in Tokyo was designed by Herzog & de Meuron.

Prada has received many honors for her contributions to international fashion. In 2004, the Council of Fashion Designers of America presented her with its International Award and in 2005 *Time* magazine named her one of the 100 most influential people in the world.

MIUCCIA PRADA

Born 1949

MILAN (ITALY)

FRANCO MOSCHINO

1950 – 1994

ABBIATEGRASSO (ITALY)

FRANCO MOSCHINO

The artist without limits

The zany, subversive fashion designer Franco Moschino was an artist without limits. Although he began as a painter and fashion illustrator, he came up with outrageous ideas during his brief career as a fashion designer in the 1980s. Moschino attended the Marangoni Fashion Institute in Milan, but since he lacked skill in hands-on dressmaking techniques, he drew sketches for his staff to complete. He always said that he was not a designer, but a painter and decorator.

Moschino delighted in ridiculing the excesses of the 1980s with whimsical appliques, logos, and slogans, and he loved visual puns. A true innovator, the suits and dresses he designed were wearable and well-cut. In 1983, he designed a dinner suit with a knife and fork appliqued on the bodice. His polka dot Minnie Mouse dresses are famous to this day. He molded dozens of miniature teddy bears into hats and scarves. He had the words "This is a Waist of Money" embroidered where the traditional gold chain belt would have been at the waist of a Chanel suit.

Moschino began sketching ideas for two Milanese fashion houses before launching his ready-to-wear line. Initially he produced jeans and daywear. His runway shows were always theatrical and irreverent; his objective was to astound the audience and fashion critics. He designed shirts made with hundreds of ties, suits with pinwheels instead of buttons, and single-sleeved shirts. The back of a man's jacket featured the words "For Fashion Victims Only."

Moschino's final runway show in 1993 was a ten-year retrospective titled *X Years of Kaos*, featuring a grand finale that filled the stage with men, women, and children dressed in white and wearing AIDS ribbons. When he died in 1994, it was reported that he died of complications from an abdominal tumor. After his death, the Moschino label has continued under various designers with American designer Jeremy Scott at the helm until 2023, continuing the tradition of Moschino's over-the-top sense of humor in dress.

JEAN PAUL GAULTIER

Born 1952

PARIS (FRANCE)

JEAN PAUL GAULTIER

The enfant terrible of French couture

In his teens, Jean Paul Gaultier spent his days creating costume sketches and fashion illustrations. Even though he would one day be called the *enfant terrible* of French couture, he was so shy that his mother accompanied him to an appointment with Pierre Cardin in 1970. Cardin hired him as an assistant on the spot.

In 1976, he presented his debut collection, then created his namesake couture and ready-to-wear label in 1982. The French designer quickly established himself, creating signature looks that blended traditional French streetwear together with haute couture. Gaultier's visual themes include variations on the marinière, the iconic blue and white striped shirt worn by French sailors, along with corseted looks reminiscent of Folies Bergère showgirls. Gaultier elevated the common with masterful tailoring and couture fabrication that made him a favorite among celebrities including Madonna, who wore his iconic pink velvet cone bra corset for her Blonde Ambition tour in 1990.

Throughout his career, Gaultier played with gender norms in his collections, blending masculine and feminine elements: men in skirts, women in men's power suits. Multicultural references also play a part of Gaultier's philosophy from Imperial Indian motifs to the Orthodox Jewish wardrobe, all with a joyful twist. Early on, Gaultier brought a diverse cast of models to his runway shows, regularly including older models with silver hair and full-figured women.

His fragrances and perfumes have been popular since their introduction, noted as bold and youthful, with distinctive bottles in male and female forms packaged in tin cans.

He also has styled fashions for films including *The Cook, the Thief, His Wife & Her Lover*, *The Fifth Element*, *City of Lost Children*, and many films for Pedro Almodóvar. Gaultier designed collections for 50 years and announced his retirement in 2020. Yet he still remains the smiling and mischievous crown prince of bad boys in fashion.

MARTIN MARGIELA

The avant-garde designer known for his experimental work

While his name is famous in the fashion world, the man is not. Martin Margiela is as much an enigma as the empty labels stitched in white thread inside his garments. He challenged the traditional practices of ready-to-wear and what luxury dress meant in the late 1980s. He was unconventional and saw fashion as an art form, embracing grunge, deconstruction, recycling, raw finishes, and oversized jackets.

Margiela graduated from Antwerp's Royal Academy of Fine Arts in 1980 and is known for his experimental, deconstructed designs, artisanal collections, and ready-to-wear. Refusing to grant most interview requests, he has avoided the public eye and succeeded at maintaining a low profile. After his runway shows, he has been known to remain behind the scenes at such unusual places as a laundry room, a Metro stop, and, in 1992, at a nearby playground.

He established Maison Martin Margiela together with Jenny Meirens in 1988. In 1994, Maison Margiela debuted its first garments, with a line of "complete reproductions," after building its collection entirely from archives. Maison Margiela's runway shows were notable in that the models' faces were often obscured by hoods, fabric, or long hair in order to direct attention toward the clothes.

In 1998, his Paris-based design company produced the infamous split-toe Tabi boots, women's wear, menswear, accessories, perfume, housewares, and his diffusion line, MM6. Margiela repurposed a leather butcher's apron into a seductive evening gown, and an old net dress into several tailored jackets. He has produced other garments with unconventional materials, including clothes fashioned from wire coat hangers, trouser suits made from 1970s upholstery fabrics, and tops made with leather gloves. In 2014, he left his company to designer John Galliano, with Margiela advising Galliano to "make it your own."

Margiela now creates art, and in 2021, his first solo show of 40 works, including sculpture, collages and paintings, which he described as "in flux, unfinished, and in permanent movement," was exhibited in Paris.

MARTIN MARGIELA

Born 1957

GENK (BELGIUM)

DRIES VAN NOTEN

The cerebral designer

Dries Van Noten is considered one of the world's most cerebral designers. Born into a Belgian family of garment makers and traders, his father owned a menswear shop and his grandfather worked as a tailor. As a child he accompanied his father to see collections in Milan and Paris, where he learned about the commercial and technical aspects of the profession.

Van Noten's education at Antwerp's Royal Academy of Fine Arts convinced him that fashion design would be a more gratifying path to follow. In 1986, he and his classmates showed their first collections in London, and Van Noten presented his first menswear collection as part of the "Antwerp Six" collective. Van Noten freelanced for various manufacturers before establishing his namesake label, quickly gaining recognition for his unique and distinctive designs. Van Noten's ready-to-wear designs are characterized by colorful prints, elaborate embroidery, original fabrics, layering, and references to ethnic patterns and textiles. His garments for men and women fuse and balance beauty and function.

Despite being known for his unique and innovation designs, Van Noten is also recognized for his commitment to sustainability. Aware of the impact of fashion on the environment, Van Noten has featured recycled materials in his collections, and has spoken openly about the need for more sustainable practices in the industry.

Van Noten draws inspiration from a range of sources, including art, music, and literature, and often incorporates these themes into his designs. He has said initial ideas can emerge "on a walk in my garden, encountering a painting or the life and work of an artist. It can be a photograph in a book, a re-read passage in a book, or a piece of music." Previous collections have been inspired by the work of iconic designer Cristóbal Balenciaga and by the art of David Bowie.

Today, Van Noten's designs are sold worldwide and he continues to create innovative collections that delight the fashion world.

DRIES VAN NOTEN

Born 1958

ANTWERP (BELGIUM)

DOMENICO DOLCE & STEFANO GABBANA

The Italian power duo

Domenico Dolce and Stefano Gabbana are the luxury fashion house team known as Dolce & Gabbana. Gabbana is a trained designer whereas Dolce worked as a tailor at an early age. The two met in the 1980s while working for a designer in Milan, where they refined their art. In 1985, with little money, they introduced their first ready-to-wear collection with friends as models.

Although Domenico and Stefano separated as a couple, they continue as a design duo. Their designs celebrate Italian culture, history, art, the church and religious motifs, Italian folk costumes, and Italian films and crafts. They constantly reinterpret *la dolce vita* with endless imagination. Their couture line is detailed, festive, feminine, and elaborate, including their signature "Sicilian Dress."

Their fashions for men and women are always glamorous and sexy. They have been inspired by thrift shop purchases and richly colored animal prints. Their menswear line conveys a macho aesthetic, with dark suits, contrasting lace shirts and embroidery. Influences inform their designs inspired by tropes of the tough guy, the gigolo, and the clergyman.

Dolce & Gabbana remains one of the most successful Italian brands, with shoes, eyewear, accessories, sport lines, perfume, fragrances, and home goods. Their fashion shows are grand and sumptuous. Attending one can feel like a glorious Italian festival, the best opera come to life, with their wearable fantasy of fashion design and gloriously detailed garments.

DOMENICO DOLCE

Born 1958

POLIZZI GENEROSA (ITALY)

STEFANO GABBANA

Born 1962

MILAN (ITALY)

ANN DEMEULEMEESTER

The avant-garde deconstructionist

Born Ann Verhelst and known professionally as Ann Demeulemeester, she first studied painting before pursuing a career in fashion design. Intrigued by what the models she painted wore, Demeulemeester shifted her focus to fashion design and graduated from Antwerp's Royal Academy of Fine Arts in 1981. Part of the visionary design group known as the "Antwerp Six," a radical and distinctive group of Belgian designers in the 1980s recognized throughout the world as avant-garde deconstructionists, she showed her first collection in London in 1986.

Demeulemeester began working as a freelance patternmaker before launching her own label. Her designs quickly gained recognition for their avant-garde and edgy style, incorporating elements of punk, androgyny, and deconstruction.

She aimed to create severe yet romantic clothing and gained inspiration from poet and singer/songwriter Patti Smith. In 1988, Demeulemeester added shoes and accessories to her collections. Critics raved about her spring 1992 collection presented at Paris Fashion Week. With its destructive edge, the avant-garde punk style featured a feminine side to its strict design.

Black and white were her favorite colors. Her presentations were never thematic but balanced between masculinity and femininity, with a sense of anarchy. She communicated concepts through clothing as she continued her search for shapes, structures, and combinations of materials.

Demeulemeester created fashions until 2013, when she turned her talents to gardening and pottery, furniture, and lighting. She studied porcelain making, and in 2019, designed and launched Ann Demeulemeester Serax, which included a collection of hand-painted porcelain dinnerware, as well as silverware, glasses, and other houseware. In 2021, she announced her return to the Ann Demeulemeester label.

ANN DEMEULEMEESTER

Born 1959

KORTRIJK (BELGIUM)

ISABEL TOLEDO

1960 – 2019

CAMAJUANÍ (CUBA)

RUBEN TOLEDO

Born 1961

HAVANA (CUBA)

ISABEL & RUBEN TOLEDO

The designers who embraced diversity and brought luxury to every woman

Isabel Toledo and her husband and creative partner, Ruben Toledo, were one of the most talented and big-hearted design teams in New York. Isabel was the fashion designer and Ruben her collaborator as well as a gifted fashion illustrator, sculptor, and mannequin designer. Sadly, breast cancer took Isabel's life far too soon.

The two were born in Cuba and grew up in New Jersey, where they met as teenagers. Isabel studied fashion at New York's Fashion Institute of Technology and at Parsons School of Design, but never graduated, instead leaving school to take an internship at the Costume Institute of the Metropolitan Museum of Art in 1979. She introduced her first collection in a night club and in 1985 as part of New York's Fashion Week.

Isabel didn't sketch. Instead, she used construction as a point of departure, working closely with Ruben to give her visions shape. Isabel insisted that she was not a fashion designer rather "a seamstress" engaged in the technique of creating clothes. She strived to incorporate a "feeling of joy in movement into the clothes [she] made for women," as she wrote in her autobiography.

Isabel was known for her sense of elegance, fascinating creation of materials, and attention to craftsmanship and simplicity. Michelle Obama was among her clients, wearing a memorable lemongrass yellow wool and lace shift dress with matching coat that Isabel created for her for President Obama's 2009 inauguration.

Isabel promoted diversity through her clothing and she worked to design for a wide audience. In addition to her work creating clothing under her own name, she served as creative director of the mass market label Anne Klein from 2006-2007. She also designed a plus-size collection for Lane Bryant in 2014.

Toledo Studio, which Isabel and Ruben ran together, received a National Design Award from the Cooper Hewitt Smithsonian Design Museum in 2005 for their work in fashion. Isabel was the subject of a retrospective at the Fashion Institute of Technology in 2009, *Isabel Toledo: Fashion From the Inside Out*.

JOHN GALLIANO

Born 1960

GIBRALTAR

JOHN GALLIANO

The fashion maverick

Growing up in London, John Galliano's mother inspired his bold and creative sensibilities. Galliano studied at St Martin's School of Art (later known as Central Saint Martins), graduating in 1984 with a first-class honors degree in fashion design. For his end of year collection, he cut clothes that could be worn inside out, upside down, by both men and women. He described the collection as "very androgynous, but huge romantic blouses with tricolors and hems that rolled up and were split." Inspired by the French Revolution, the collection was immediately purchased by Browns fashion boutique in London.

That same year, he established his own label, which was simpler and more feminine, but financial concerns forced him to abandon his early vision. In 1989, a generous patron contributed finances for him to rebuild his label. He created the first collection from just one bolt of fabric.

Galliano was the first British designer to work for a house of haute couture when he designed for Givenchy from 1995-1996. He designed for the house of Christian Dior from 1996-2011 where he was known for his flamboyant and daring designs that redefined the brand. He drew inspiration from diverse sources, including haute couture, street fashion, historical dress, and ethnic and tribal styles.

Since 2014, he has overseen the design for avant-garde label Maison Margiela, where he presented his first couture collection in 2015. Always a showman, Galliano created some of the industry's most famous collections and was infamous for the end of show bow when he would step out dressed in a uniform inspired by Napoleon or as an American astronaut.

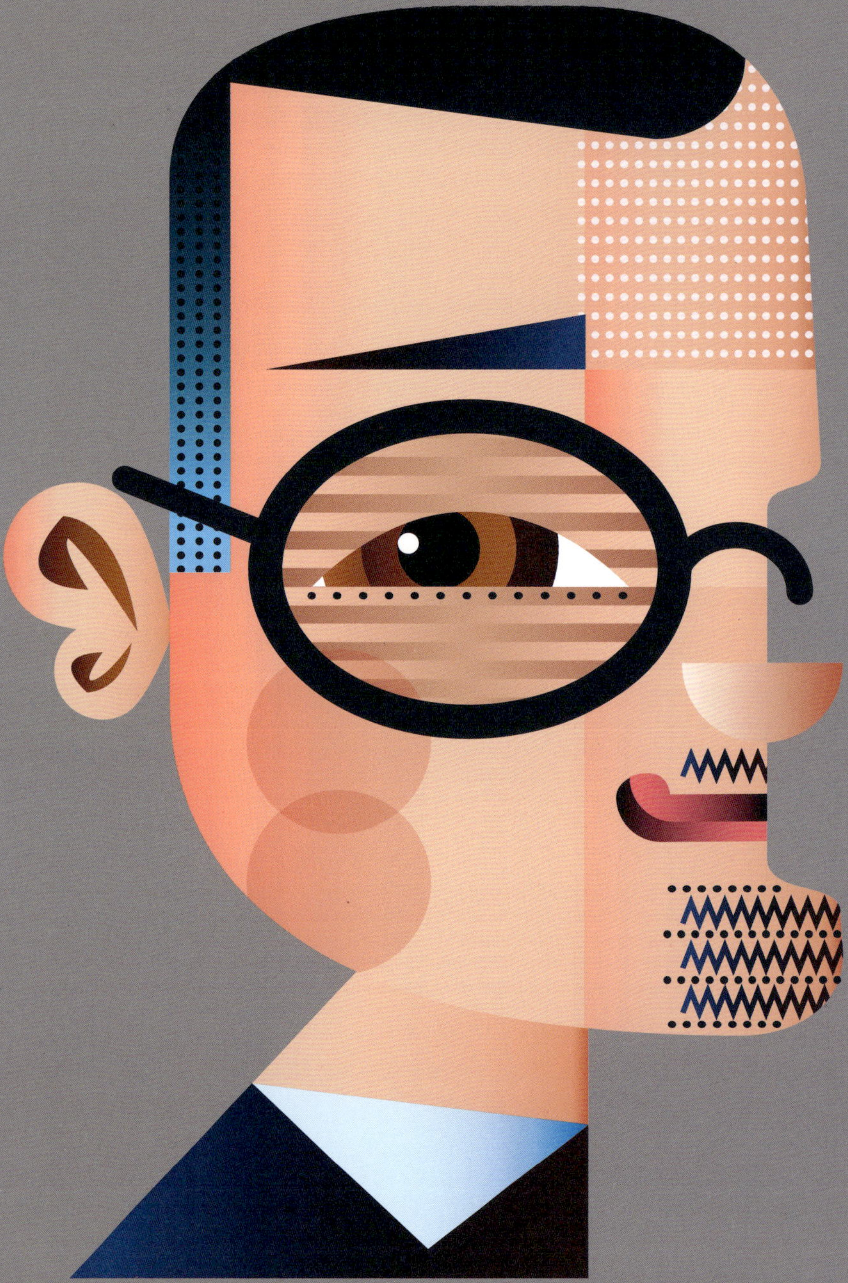

JUNYA WATANABE

Born 1961

FUKUSHIMA (JAPAN)

JUNYA WATANABE

The experimental designer

Junya Watanabe is an avant-garde fashion designer who lives and works in Tokyo. Born in Fukushima, he has said that nothing really made him want to start creating clothes, other than the fact that his mother operated a made-to-order clothing store. He graduated from Tokyo's Bunka Fashion College in 1984. At the same time, he began apprenticing as a pattern cutter at Comme de Garçons, and in 1987, he designed for Comme des Garçons Homme.

In 1992, he established his own line as part of the company, Junya Watanabe Comme des Garçons. The following year he began showing his line four times a year in Paris. He has never taken a bow at the end of his fashion shows.

Fashion journalists describe the designer as intellectual. His clothes are complicated to make and to wear, yet intriguing. His experimental designs emerge from continually reconfiguring existing garments. A 1999 runway show featured fabrics that become waterproof when reversed, demonstrated by an isolated "cloudburst" that showered rain over the models, mid-runway during the show. He introduced his Techno-culture collection, including innovative, structured fabrics in 2000.

In 2007, Converse hired Watanabe to design a series of shoes. He has also collaborated with Levi-Strauss, Carhartt, Nike, and The North Face. He designed a remote-control toy car for the Tamiya Corporation and in 2016, Watanabe developed a solar-powered jacket for his menswear line.

Watanabe's pieces look like nothing we have ever seen before. He works with what he calls "dumb" clothes: trench coats, biker jackets, the white shirt, and totally repurposes them, ripping garments apart.

"It all begins inside my head," he says. "I start to look for strings of ideas that interest me."

ALBER ELBAZ

The fashion philosopher

Born in Morocco, Alber Elbaz was raised in Israel and moved to New York in the early 1980s to pursue his dreams of a career in the fashion industry. While in New York, Elbaz worked with designer Geoffrey Beene, where he honed his design skills and developed a keen sense of style.

Elbaz relocated to Paris in the late 1990s, first designing for French fashion house Guy Laroche and then worked as creative director at legendary French design house Lanvin. One of the oldest couture houses in Paris, Elbaz successfully rejuvenated the label as its head for nearly 15 years.

Elbaz's designs for Lanvin were inspired by a sense of playfulness and whimsy. When wearing his fashions, clients believed they were in his joyful presence. His couture was light in aesthetics, comfortable, and slightly eccentric. His fashions were classic with a difference, beautiful and functional. He created silk cocktail dresses and other feminine designs, often playing with color or other unusual variations on hallmark elegance. Elbaz was known for his use of bold colors, luxurious fabrics, and unexpected details, like ruffles, bows, and sequins.

A rarity in the fashion world, Elbaz was well-respected for his compassion and generosity among coworkers. One fashion critic remembered that he always conducted himself as a gracious gentleman. Another admirer considered him a fashion philosopher. Unfortunately, Elbaz's life was cut short when he died of complications from Covid-19 at the age of 59. He continues to be remembered as one of the most beloved fashion designers by both his clients and peers.

ALBER ELBAZ

1961 – 2021

CASABLANCA (MOROCCO)

TOM FORD

Born 1961

AUSTIN, TEXAS (USA)

TOM FORD

The designer with the Midas touch

Legendary American designer Tom Ford has made a name for himself as an influential creative force in the fashion industry. After studying architecture at Parsons School of Design, he began his career in fashion working for sportswear designer Cathy Hardwick, and then for the Perry Ellis label.

In 1990, Ford moved to Italy to design women's wear for Gucci, and soon added responsibility for menswear, shoes, fragrance, accessories, marketing, advertising, and store design. Working 18-hour days during his time as Gucci's creative director, Ford successfully modernized the struggling brand.

Ford's dresses were refined, spare and luxurious as in his return of a man's velvet jacket. He delivered successive collections referring in style to the disco era of the 1970s. Ford's menswear showcased strong, clean, masculine aesthetics.

In 1999, Ford moved to Paris to design for Yves Saint Laurent after the house was acquired by Gucci. As design director, he rejuvenated the label to be more contemporary. His fragrance advertisements were daring and risqué.

In 2005, Ford introduced his own luxury label, Tom Ford, creating bold, confident fashions hugging the body with clean and simple sophisticated tailoring. He included eyewear and men's grooming products. Ford's aesthetic is in everything he does—seductive, desirable, alluring, provocative and sensual. His aesthetic has been described as "Hollywood glamour mixed with everyday wearability." One of the most successful individuals in fashion, he is an architect of luxurious clothing.

Ford's work has garnered praise from the fashion industry, winning numerous CFDA awards during his career. He also successfully branched out into the film world, garnering critical praise as a director for his work on the Oscar-nominated *A Single Man* and *Nocturnal Animals*.

RICK OWENS

The rule breaker with a bold vision

Today, designer Rick Owens can be spotted wearing his usual black monk-like garb in either Paris, where he moved in 2003, or Venice, where he has had a second home since 2014.

Owens studied at Otis College of Art and Design in Los Angeles, then took courses at the Los Angeles Trade-Technical College, where he learned draping and patternmaking. In 1994, he established his namesake label, creating apparel exclusively for Charles Gallay, a luxury retailer in Los Angeles that promotes avant-garde designers. Together with his wife and muse Michelle Lamy, he founded Owenscorp, an art and furniture company, in 2004.

Known for his experimental and avant-garde approach to fashion, Owens's designs are edgy and unconventional. His runway shows run the gamut from low-key to elaborately staged set pieces. In 1998, the Rick Owens collection featured draping and the bias cut in his materials of choice—silk, leather, and fur. The collection is noteworthy as the models were all transgender personalities and sex workers. In 2013, his Prehistoric collection comprised seven pieces in a palette sliding from white to black. The title referred to the beginnings of humanity, recalling an ancient civilization. He shocked critics with his menswear Sphinx collection with clothing designed to reveal male models' genitals, inspired by classical marble sculptures.

His labels include Rick Owens, Rickowneslilies, and Hunrickowens. In 2005, Drkshdw was established as a diffusion line consisting of basic garments with distressed finishings, oil washing, and wax coatings.

His bold vision has earned Owens acclaim from the fashion industry. He has won the Cooper-Hewitt Design Award, the International Rule Breaker Award, and both the Lifetime Achievement Award and the Menswear Designer of the Year from the CFDA. The first museum retrospective of his work, featuring 20 years of design, *Subhuman, Inhuman, Superhuman*, opened at the Triennale di Milano in 2017.

RICK OWENS

Born 1962

PORTERVILLE, CALIFORNIA (USA)

MARC JACOBS

The designer who epitomized New York style

As the perennial tough kid of fashion, Marc Jacobs continues to innovate and was among the first designers to establish streetwise aesthetics: "a mix of a little preppie, a little grunge, a little couture." He creates well-tailored clothing that straddles high-end femininity and streetwear. His city-inspired looks are edgy yet charming, wicked yet elegant.

As a teen, Jacobs lived with his grandmother on New York's Upper West Side and she guided his focus to fashion. He attended Manhattan's High School of Art and Design and studied at Parsons School of Design. At only 21 years old, he designed his first collection for the label Sketchbook.

In 1986, Jacobs debuted his first collection with the Marc Jacobs label. In 1987, he was the youngest designer to receive the Council of Fashion Designers Award for New Fashion Talent. He won the CFDA prize for Womenswear Designer of the Year in both 1992 and 1997, and in 2002 was named the Menswear Designer of the Year.

In 1989, Jacobs joined Perry Ellis to oversee its women's wear line but was dismissed in 1993 after he designed his grunge collection. The following year, he established Marc Jacobs International, which included a menswear collection. His lower-priced Marc by Marc Jacobs line launched in 2001.

As Louis Vuitton's creative director from 1997-2014, he injected a new creative mojo into the venerable house of luxury, introducing the first ready-to-wear line in the company's long history. Jacobs was among the first to embrace the concept of collaborations, working with guest artists on products featuring Stephen Sprouse's day-glow neon graffiti and Richard Prince's artistic brush strokes. Louis Vuitton's "must-have" luxury handbag achieved pop icon status with Takashi Murakami's floral animé characters among the LV logo.

With his timeless sense of style and remarkable ability to know what is cool, Jacobs continues to be the fashion designer of not only right now, but the future.

MARC JACOBS

Born 1963

NEW YORK, NEW YORK (USA)

DURO OLOWU

Born 1965

LAGOS (NIGERIA)

DURO OLOWU

Fashion's renaissance man

The London based-fashion designer Duro Olowu was born in Lagos, Nigeria, to a Jamaican mother and Nigerian father. Raised between Nigeria and England, he was brought up in an environment that embraced international culture, art, fashion, and music. Since the age of six, he has sketched design ideas, inspired by his mother and his cousins' play clothes.

Olowu moved to London at the age of 16 and later earned a law degree at the University of Kent, although he realized that his passion was fashion design. A self-taught designer, he is a master of tailoring, giving attention to details. His designs incorporate a kaleidoscope of neon-accented zigzag prints, West African motifs, and florals.

He introduced his first collection in 2004, which included the "Duro dress" with its empire waist and billowing sleeves in vibrant mixed silk prints. It was an immediate success and was hailed by *Vogue* as the dress of the year. Olowu brings a sense of his expansive world view, incorporating a design past while bringing his works forward into ready-to-wear.

Michelle Obama is a client and has chosen to wear Olowu's fashions since 2015. As First Lady, Obama commissioned Olowu to decorate a room in the White House. Olowu said he envisioned "a backdrop for a magical and surrealistic festive atmosphere."

Olowu has earned widespread recognition for his work. In 2005, he won the New Designer of the Year award at the British Fashion Awards. In 2009, he was named the Best International Designer at the African Fashion Awards. He was included in the 2019, 2020 and 2021 editions of the Powerlist, a compendium of each year's 100 most influential Black Britons.

A true renaissance man, Olowu has expanded into the world of art curation, selecting and presenting the work of a range of contemporary artists in galleries and museums around the world.

THOM BROWNE

The expert tailor with an American sensibility

Raised in a family with seven siblings, designer Thom Browne found early influences from his childhood love of sports. An avid athlete, Browne attended the University of Notre Dame, graduating with a degree in economics, before moving to New York to pursue a career in fashion.

Browne got his start working retail for Armani but found his true calling when he landed a job at Club Monaco where he designed their menswear collections. After several years, Browne left to start his eponymous label Thom Browne.

He began with a few hand-tailored suits displayed in a made-to-measure shop. Each sharply tailored suit coordinated with a grey cardigan, white Oxford-cloth shirt, grey necktie, and classic footwear. His tailored grey suit is elemental to all he does. Known for a slim fit, his suit pants often have tapered, cropped legs; he has also paired suit jackets with shorts and kilts. Browne continually redefines tailoring for menswear and women's wear, conveying a true American style. He has a commitment to outstanding fabric selections and tailoring. To Browne, uniformity conveys confidence.

Browne incorporates horizontal stripes in his menswear, influenced by his love of sports and the uniforms worn by athletes. His signature red, white, and blue grosgrain is the brand's visual identifier. His signature four-stripe design can be seen on everything from neckties to socks.

In 2021, Adidas sued Browne's company for infringing on the use of Adidas stripes. Adidas complained that customers could confuse Browne's four-stripe design with Adidas's three parallel stripes. Browne's attorney prevailed, contending that there is no competition since Thom Browne is a luxury brand, and Adidas is a sports brand.

THOM BROWNE

Born 1965

ALLENTOWN, PENNSYLVANIA (USA)

HEDI SLIMANE

The designer who disrupted menswear with his skinny aesthetic

Growing up in France, Italian-Tunisian Hedi Slimane was interested in music and photography at an early age and was also surrounded by fashion. His mother was a dressmaker and two of his uncles were tailors. As a child, he and his mother would shop for fabrics and make clothes together. Concerned that a career in the fashion industry would be too competitive, Slimane studied art history at the Ecole du Louvre. He completed an apprenticeship at a menswear design house, although like many of his peers, he has no formal training in fashion design.

In 1996, Slimane was hired as ready-to-wear director of men's collections at Yves Saint Laurent where he would later become artistic director. In 2002, he joined the house of Christian Dior as creative director of Dior Homme. At the same time, he introduced Dior's first men's fragrance, Higher. Slimane disrupted the menswear fashion industry when he introduced his androgynous "skinny" silhouette, blending traditional tailoring with a rock and roll feel.

In 2007, Slimane left Dior to pursue his passion for photography. His work was well received and has been exhibited in galleries internationally. He photographed campaigns for fashion brands, including Saint Laurent, Prada, and Chanel, while also creating album covers for rock bands, including Phoenix.

Slimane eventually returned to the world of fashion as creative director of Yves Saint Laurent, and in 2018, took on the role of creative director at Celine. He is known for his minimalist approach to fashion and signature black-and-white aesthetic. Among his clients are celebrities including Madonna, Lady Gaga, and Rihanna.

Throughout his career, Slimane has been praised for his innovative designs, as well as his ability to innovate in both the fashion and photography worlds, winning numerous awards. In 2002, he became the first menswear designer to receive the CFDA's International Designer of the Year award.

HEDI SLIMANE

Born 1968

PARIS (FRANCE)

ALEXANDER McQUEEN

1969 – 2010

LONDON, ENGLAND (UK)

ALEXANDER McQUEEN

The designer with a flair for drama

Lee Alexander McQueen, known as Lee to friends and Alexander McQueen professionally, was a British fashion designer and couturier. His life was cut short when he tragically committed suicide in 2010.

McQueen's reputation for tailoring was exemplary and well-earned. Years before earning his master's degree in fashion from London's Central Saint Martins, he honed his tailoring skills as an apprentice coat maker and pattern cutter for several tailors in London's Savile Row.

McQueen's designs explored themes such as romanticism, sexuality, and death, including collections that incorporated autobiographical elements. He had a flair for drama, orchestrating provocative, often controversial, highly theatrical fashion shows that shocked audiences with effects such as two robots spray painting a model dressed in his latest avant-garde design. McQueen's first collection for his own label introduced a pair of trousers named "bumsters"—very low-rise jeans intentionally designed to reveal the cleavage of the derrière.

In 1996, McQueen was named creative director for the French fashion house Givenchy, where he toned his rebellious nature with a first collection inspired by Greek mythology. McQueen's relationship with Givenchy was tumultuous, and he left when his contract expired in 2001.

He simultaneously designed under his namesake label, creating very dark, romantic looks, incorporating streamlined silhouettes, needlework, beading, fresh flowers, and in particular, deer antlers. Among his most memorable designs are the iconic skull scarf and armadillo shoes.

He received the British Designer of the Year award in 1996 and was appointed Commander of the Order of the British Empire in 2003. He received the CFDA's International Designer of the Year award the same year. After his death, collaborator Sarah Burton took over as creative director of the label, continuing his fashion legacy.

VIKTOR HORSTING
Born 1969
GELDROP (NETHERLANDS)

ROLF SNOEREN
Born 1969
DONGEN (NETHERLANDS)

VIKTOR HORSTING & ROLF SNOEREN

Dutch designers who bring an intellectual flair and sense of literature to their creations

Two Dutch visionaries who continue to challenge fashion audiences, Viktor Horsting and Rolf Snoeren met as art students at the Arnhem Academy of Art and Design in the Netherlands. Together, they co-founded the fashion house Viktor&Rolf in 1993. Since their start, they have aimed to bridge the divide between fashion and art.

Their early work featured silhouettes inspired by the classic houses of Dior and Chanel, but with their own variations. Their first collection was criticized in the fashion world and it wasn't until 1998, when they presented their first haute couture collection during Fashion Week, that they had their breakthrough. Their designs were bold and included asymmetrical tailoring, and a multitude of drapes and folds. Their first ready-to-wear collection debuted in 2000 and had a couture-like attitude.

Viktor&Rolf is known for its avant-garde concepts, and runway shows are legendary, conceived before the design process begins. In the late 1990s, they fitted all the dresses and outfits from the collection on just one model, known as the Russian Doll collection. A 2019 runway show featured elaborate gowns with large political messages and pop culture slogans. One collection returned to their love of pleated starched tulle, but with upside down and sideways, gravity-defying dresses. They have presented moving images projected onto the bodies of unmoving models and sent tap-dancing models down the runway.

To Viktor&Rolf, presentation is everything. Proud of its Dutch heritage, the duo often references the paintings of the Dutch old masters by incorporating the iconic ruff collar into designs with starched tulle pleated fabric.

Horsting and Snoeren dress as mirror images of each other, so they appear as mismatched fraternal twins. Two smart, playful designers, their work is always moving towards the new, intellectual, questioning, and brilliant.

NICOLAS GHESQUIÈRE

Born 1971

COMINES (FRANCE)

NICOLAS GHESQUIÈRE

The designer who turned Balenciaga into the house of the future

Nicolas Ghesquière began sketching dresses as a bored teen on a family holiday. By the age of 12, the already innovative Ghesquière was fabricating dresses from his mother's curtains and designing earrings from his grandmother's chandelier crystals. With his father's help, he compiled a portfolio of his designs and secured a fashion internship with agnès b., the Paris-based luxury clothing company, at the age of 15.

Ghesquière did not study at art school so that he could begin working as an assistant to French fashion designer Jean Paul Gaultier. When he was just 25 years old, he was appointed creative director at Balenciaga, and began to turn the antiquated fashion house into the house of now. Ghesquière reinvented the classic Balenciaga silhouette and his work was praised as futuristic. He became known for his contrasting fashions that created a new tailored look: boxy blouses with tight skinny pants, or a tightly cut jumpsuit with voluminous sleeves. His biggest commercial success was the brand's Lariat bag, an unstructured purse with braided handles and dangling zipper pulls. With no visible logo, it became one of the defining accessories of the mid-2000s. Ghesquière's 15 years at Balenciaga were a success, growing the company and reestablishing the house for contemporary fashion with his exciting, bold, confident looks.

Following his departure from Balenciaga, Ghesquière became the director of women's fashion for Louis Vuitton. He has continued to push fashion forward with his bold and futuristic designs, blending motorcycle jackets with short, ruffled skirts, playing with different cuts and fabrics, and fusing the new with the elegant. Ghesquière has been called the future of fashion for his modern and innovative work.

STELLA McCARTNEY

The designer who made cruelty-free fashions luxurious

Born to world-famous creative parents, Stella McCartney's childhood was filled with music, art, travel, and creativity. Her father, Sir Paul McCartney, was a member of The Beatles, and her mother, Linda, was a gifted photographer and animal activist. Young Stella's passion for fashion design began at the age of 13 when she designed her first jacket. She then went on to study fashion design at Central Saint Martins in London.

After graduating, she joined Chloé as creative director, a position she held for four years, before leaving to start her namesake fashion label. Known for creating sustainable and ethical fashion, McCartney's label gained recognition for its easygoing yet chic style that appealed to the modern woman. McCartney is known for her bold and modern silhouettes, playful prints, and eco-friendly materials. Her collaboration with Adidas on a women's sportswear collection attracted worldwide acclaim.

An advocate for animal rights and veganism, McCartney has never used leather, feathers, fur, or skin in her designs, proving that it is possible to create beautiful, cruelty-free products. She uses her platform to support many charitable organizations, including Greenpeace and PETA. She also co-founded Meat Free Monday, an environmental campaign that aims to reduce meat consumption and promote a more plant-based diet.

McCartney has been honored with many awards, including an Office of the Order of the British Empire for her services to fashion. Her innovative approach to fashion and dedication to sustainability have made McCartney an influential designer in the industry today, and her global fashion brand continues to grow, with flagship stores in major fashion cities worldwide.

STELLA McCARTNEY

Born 1971

LONDON, ENGLAND (UK)

PHOEBE PHILO

Born 1973

PARIS (FRANCE)

PHOEBE PHILO

The queen of minimalist chic

Designer Phoebe Philo expressed an interest in fashion design at a young age and began customizing her clothes after her parents gave her a sewing machine for her 14th birthday. Today, she is known for elegance and modernism. Many of her designs are created with herself in mind, designing essentials that she would want to wear.

After graduating from Central Saint Martins in London, she worked as Stella McCartney's assistant at Chloé. When McCartney left Chloé in 2001, Philo stepped into the role of creative director. Under Philo's creative leadership, Chloé became a commercial success. She is credited with ushering in the trends of baby-doll dresses and heavy leather accessories, like Chloé's instantly recognizable Paddington bag.

In 2008, when Philo was appointed creative director at the Paris-based design house Celine, it was on the condition that she and her designers work from London. Philo successfully reinvigorated the French label with her minimalist aesthetic, clean lines, and tonal color palettes. Her collections for Celine focused on wearable clothing that was minimal, yet luxurious and practical, rooted in reality.

Shifting her priorities to nurture and cultivate her family life, Philo was the first designer at a major fashion house to take an extended maternity leave when her first child was born. In 2018, Philo stepped away from Celine to take a sabbatical. In 2021, she announced the launch of her own namesake label focusing on "clothing and accessories rooted in exceptional quality and design."

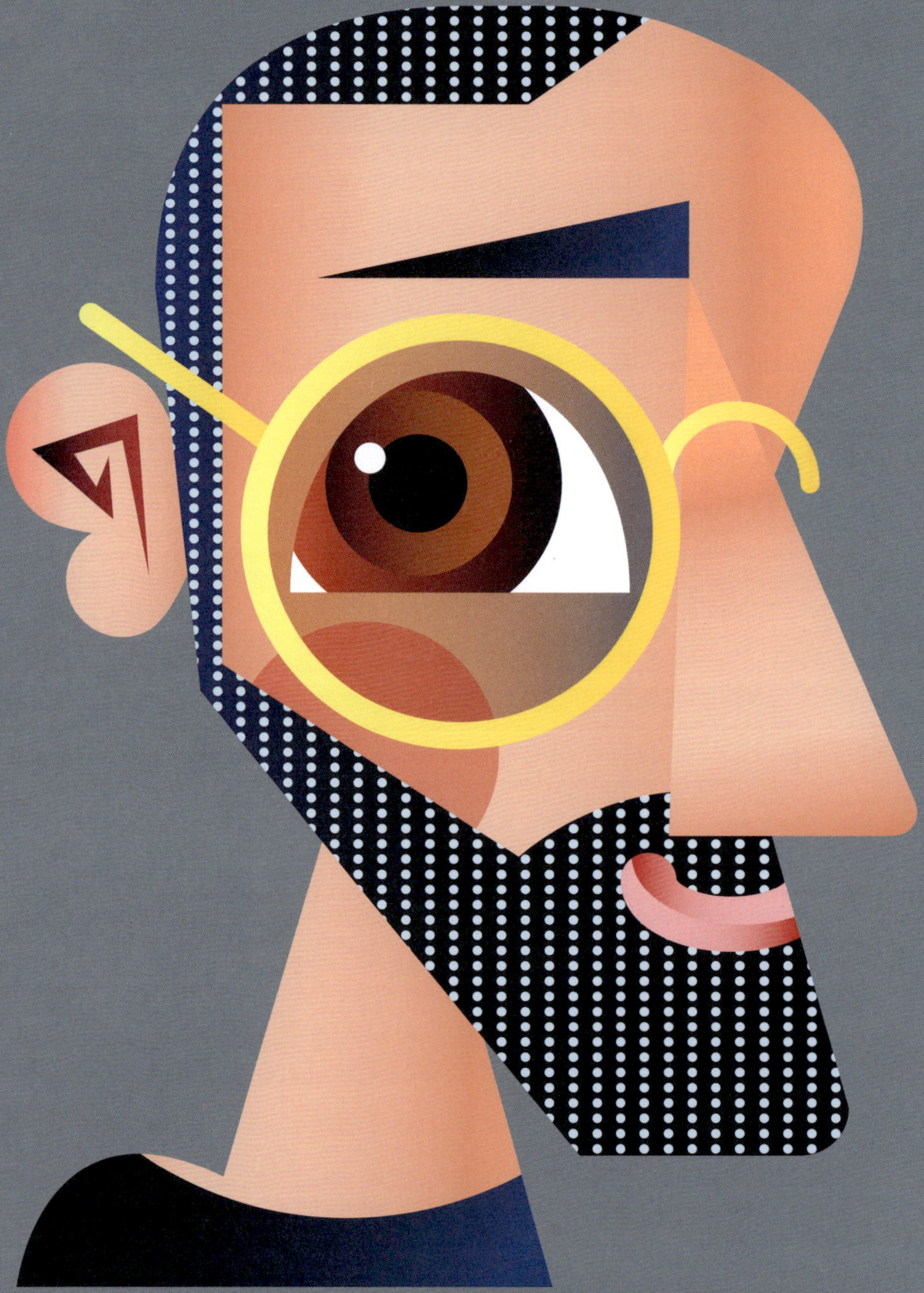

RABIH KAYROUZ

Born 1973

LEBANON

RABIH KAYROUZ

The Lebanese designer with elegant taste and an undying love of his home country

Rabih Kayrouz knew from an early age that he wanted to be a fashion designer. Encouraged by his parents, Kayrouz moved to Paris at the age of 16 to study at the Chambre Syndicale de la Couture Parisienne. After finishing school, he apprenticed in the fashion houses of Chanel and Dior before returning to Lebanon.

While in Beirut, Kayrouz presented his fashion work as the Salon des Artistes at an exhibition for young designers. His work was well received, and he gained recognition for designing evening gowns and wedding dresses. He had the desire to stay in Lebanon and established his couture house, Maison Rabih Kayrouz, in Beirut in 1999.

Kayrouz is known for elegant clothing, made with sumptuous fabrics, and a sensuous fluidity. He takes a modern approach to couture techniques, draping materials directly on clients. With beautiful hand tailoring, his creations are graceful, luxurious, and flowing, with almost sculpture-like forms and shapes. He pairs colors and shapes in a glorious mix of ease and his designs have an elegant restraint, yet are still playful. He designs for women of all ages, shapes, and forms, envisioning the independent, strong woman who embraces her feminine and sensual side.

Kayrouz returned to Paris and opened an atelier there in 2009, but remains committed to his home country of Lebanon, maintaining his flagship store in Beirut. He employs artisans in Lebanon through various partnerships that support underprivileged women and refugees. In addition to his couture and ready-to-wear lines, Kayrouz also designs costumes for the opera and theater productions, and with brands including Eres and La Redoute.

KATE & LAURA MULLEAVY

The designing sisters who blur the line between fashion and art

Sisters Kate and Laura Mulleavy are the design team behind American fashion brand Rodarte. After graduating from the University of California-Berkeley—Laura with a degree in English literature, Kate with a degree in art history—the Mulleavys returned home to Pasadena, California. It was there that they began to design on their parents' kitchen table. Both saved up money to create their first capsule collection of ten pieces.

With no formal training, they launched Rodarte in 2005. It was an immediate success. The sisters quickly gained notice for their meticulous approach, couture-like finishing and romantic concepts, with one chiffon dress from their 2006 collection taking 150 hours to complete.

The sibling duo is inspired by the American cultural landscape, particularly their native West coast. Their aesthetics have evolved since they began designing. Rodarte's 2010 collections were darker, riskier, and more deconstructed, with influences from punk, gothic, as well as animé and horror films. An article about Rodarte in *The New Yorker* in 2010 observed that, "People in the know really love it, but to everyone else it's inscrutable or a little bit ugly."

In addition to Rodarte, the Mulleavys collaborated on capsule collections with The Gap in 2007 and with Target in 2009. In 2010, the sisters created custom knitwear for the U.S. Olympic team. Blurring the line between fashion and art, they created costumes for the Oscar-winning film *Black Swan*, as well as for various opera productions. They have also branched out by writing and directing the film *Woodshock*, starring Kirsten Dunst.

KATE MULLEAVY
Born 1979
OAKLAND, CALIFORNIA (USA)

LAURA MULLEAVY
Born 1980
PASADENA, CALIFORNIA (USA)

VIRGIL ABLOH

1980 – 2021

ROCKFORD, ILLINOIS (USA)

VIRGIL ABLOH

The genre bending designer who was taken too soon

Virgil Abloh was not only a fashion designer, but also a multidisciplinary artist. Raised in a middle-class home by Ghanaian parents, Abloh's mother was a seamstress who taught him to sew. As a child, he was interested in hip-hop and skateboarding, and these early influences helped to shape his design aesthetic.

Abloh received his bachelor's degree in civil engineering and earned a master's degree in architecture. After graduating, he interned at Fendi alongside Kanye West. Abloh and West became friends and collaborators, and Abloh served as West's creative director for many years.

Abloh launched his first fashion label, Pyrex Vision, in 2012. He screen-printed Ralph Lauren flannel shirts with the word "Pyrex" and the number 23, Michael Jordan's number when he played basketball for the Chicago Bulls. The next year, he launched his own label, Off-White, meaning "the grey area between black and white," a fitting description of his menswear that effortlessly balanced streetwear and high fashion. Known for its tongue-in-cheek humor, Abloh's collection featured screen-printed hoodies, denim shirts, jackets, and basketball shorts.

Abloh's architecture degree provided the foundation for his expert tailoring for menswear when he served as artistic director at Louis Vuitton, the first person of color to hold that position. Abloh was credited for bringing a new energy to the brand, combining the house's signature sophistication with his own youthful, streetwear-inspired design aesthetic.

In 2019, Chicago's Museum of Contemporary Art mounted the extensive exhibition *Virgil Abloh: Figures of Speech*. The catalogue described him as "a genre bending artist and designer who pioneered a practice that cuts across media and connects visual artists." Abloh collaborated with Levi-Strauss, IKEA, and Timberland, but his best-known partnership was with Nike for a collection of redesigns of the brand's bestselling shoes. At the height of his career, Abloh's life was cut tragically short when he died of cancer at only 41 years old.

SIMONE ROCHA

Fashion's storyteller

Designer Simone Rocha was immersed in fashion at a young age. The daughter of fashion designer John Rocha, Simone believes that fashion is 100 percent of her life and is the reason she is so open-minded. Her father let young Simone work alongside him in his studio before she began her studies at the National College of Art and Design in Dublin. After graduating, she earned her Master of Arts degree from London's Central Saint Martins. The same year, she presented her first collection at the Tate Modern during Fashion Week, featuring perforated pink neoprene, traditionally used as a sports fabric, that she manipulated into little suits. "I've built my world on contradictions," commented Rocha on her diverse background.

Rocha sees her work coalescing at the intersection of fashion and art, nature, family, and Ireland. She believes that femininity runs through her collections because they are by a woman for a woman. Her work showcases an appreciation for all aspects of culture, exploring the strands of her Asian-Irish heritage. She once filled a car with dried flowers, reflecting the blend of artificial and natural elements that forms her aesthetic, which was displayed in the windows of stores in London, New York, and Hong Kong.

She believes that growing up in Ireland connects her to an earthiness, contrasting hard and soft, or man-made vs. nature. She feels that all of her fashions have stories, similar to the traditional Irish folktales.

In 2018, Rocha curated *A Magazine Curated By*, a fashion magazine that explores the universe of a chosen designer in each issue. Rocha's issue explored aesthetics through the themes of Ireland, Hong Kong, China, and family.

In 2016, Rocha was named the Womenswear Designer of the Year at the British Fashion Awards. She collaborated with Moncler in 2018, and joined forces with H&M in 2021 to celebrate her tenth anniversary, making her signature aesthetic more accessible.

SIMONE ROCHA

Born 1986

DUBLIN (IRELAND)

KERBY JEAN-RAYMOND

The designer who makes the runway a platform for social justice

Despite being one of the most exciting and groundbreaking young voices in fashion design, Kerby Jean-Raymond's life had a tumultuous start. He was born in Brooklyn in a neighborhood that was characterized by violence and was an epicenter of the crack epidemic. He lost several friends to gun violence and the prison system. Jean-Raymond became interested in fashion at an early age and initially planned to be a sneaker designer, something he achieved when he served as global creative director for Reebok from 2020-2022.

While attending Manhattan's High School of Fashion Design, he interned with Kay Unger and Marchesa, among others. Jean-Raymond graduated from Hofstra University with a business degree and began working in the corporate world, eventually returning to his fashion dreams.

He launched Pyer Moss in 2013, aiming to create a brand that blended high-end fashion with activism and social commentary. His spring 2016 menswear collection highlighted police brutality and referenced the Black Lives Matter movement. His printed silk button-down shirt with watercolor washes of blues and greens animates the black family, inspired by the artist Derrick Adams. An iconic look reveals a black cropped leather jacket with cowboy-style stitching and matching black leather pants, a black power suit.

Jean-Raymond supports fashion's ability to reshape culture and utilizes his shows to highlight black contributions to history and "end the erasure of minorities and people of color," he told the *New York Times*. He continues to address racial tensions, income inequality, and social justice in his collections. He never shies away from making political commentary and challenging social narratives in his fashions.

His designs have been worn by Rihanna, Michelle Obama, and Kamala Harris. In 2018, he received the prestigious CFDA/Vogue Fashion Fund Award, which recognizes emerging talent in the field.

KERBY JEAN-RAYMOND

Born 1986

NEW YORK, NEW YORK (USA)

FASHION
ICONS

DAVID LEE CSICSKO

DAVID LEE CSICSKO is an award-winning artist and designer. As a young artistic child, he dreamed of traveling to Paris, illustrating books, living the artist's life, and working on fashion projects for Chicago's famous Marshall Fields department store. And as a young man, he did. His shopping bags for Bloomingdale's are part of the permanent collection of the Cooper Hewitt, Smithsonian Design Museum in New York City. He currently designs very collectible and reusable shopping bags for Mariano's grocery stores in Chicago. David's lively illustrations can also be seen in *LGBTQ+ Icons*, *Science People*, and *Iconic Composers*, the first three books of the People Series.

GILLION CARRARA

GILLION CARRARA is a Professor Adjunct in the Department of Art History, Theory and Criticism at the School of the Art institute of Chicago. In her studies, her focus is on contemporary and avant-garde fashion and dress, art, literature, and sociology. Until 2017, she was the founding Director of the Fashion Resource Center, and built a collection of contemporary and avant-garde fashion, publications and various media. She actively writes book and exhibition reviews for publication, presents lectures locally and nationally, attends costume symposiums and was on the Board of Costume Colloquium, Florence, Italy, until it's conclusion in 2020 and is a current member of the International Council of Museums (ICOM).

AESTHETIC A specific and unique concept, a look, that advises a designer when compiling their designs.

APPLIQUE A form of needlework in which smaller pieces of fabric are sewn into a pattern or picture onto a garment or larger piece of fabric.

ARTISANAL Anything considered handmade or made using traditional methods.

ASYMMETRICAL A design in which one side of clothing is not the same length as its opposing side.

ATELIER Studio or workshop used by a designer to create.

AVANT-GARDE Advocating and inciting new and experimental ideas while pushing boundaries.

BEATNIK A rebellious and non-conforming style of fashion created in the 1960s that prioritized originality and freedom of speech in their attire.

BIAS/BIAS CUT A technique used to place and cut patterns into the fabric at a 45-degree angle.

BODICE A constricting waist-length garment worn over dresses and blouses.

BOUTIQUE A small shop that sells fashionable clothing and accessories, typically offering less variety than a department store.

BROOCH A decorative ornament made with a pin on the back that can be attached to clothing.

BUSTLE A 19th-century padded undergarment used to support drapery and add fullness to the back of women's dresses.

CAFTAN A full-length garment with wide sleeves and an open chest and neckline.

CHEMISE An unrestricted undergarment usually worn to sleep in and made of silk or satin and decorated with lace trimming.

COLLECTION A curated list of clothing and accessories that can be worn together.

CORSET A fitted garment worn under clothing to help tighten and sculpt the waist and torso.

CFDA (Council of Fashion Designers of America) a not-for-profit trade association for America's leading designers in menswear, women's wear, jewelry, and accessories.

COUTURE Handmade and made-to-measure fashion.

COUTURIER A male designer that makes and sells high fashion clothing.

COUTURIERE A female designer that makes and sells high fashion clothing.

DECONSTRUCTED Garments incorporating raw edges, exposed seams, and distressed textiles that often have an unfinished appearance at the end of the design process.

DIFFUSION LINE A secondary line of goods created by higher end brands that offer lower prices, catering to a larger market.

DRAPE The placement of a fabric or garment on a model during the pinning process to help develop a more flowing structure.

EMBROIDERED To decorate cloth or clothing with embellished patterns or with stitches sewn directly into the material.

EMPIRE WAIST A style in which a dress has a fitted bodice that ends just beneath the bustline rather than the waistline, creating a high waist appearance.

ENFANT TERRIBLE An individual with controversial and outrageous behavior or a successful person who is unconventional and innovative.

ENSEMBLE A group of clothing and accessories viewed as an entire piece rather than individually.

FASHION SHOW A show to display a designer/brand's collection to potential buyers.

FASHION WEEK A week dedicated to fashion designers and brands that wish to display their latest collection, in a runway approach, to the media and buyers.

FIT & FLARE A style that cinches through the waist and flows out below the hips.

GRUNGE A style that focuses on de-emphasizing the silhouette of the body, often presenting an untidy look.

HABERDASHERY A shop selling men's clothing and accessories.

HAUTE COUTURE High fashion clothing.

HIGH-END FEMININITY Exuding expensive, exclusive, and feminine characteristics.

KIMONO A traditional Japanese garment designed as a robe with wide sleeves.

LABEL The trade name or brand of a line of clothing or accessories.

LAMPSHADE TUNIC A dress designed by Paul Poiret that features a soft bodice shape, full bat wing arms that takes emphasis away from the shoulder, and a hobble skirt.

LAPELS A piece of folded fabric on the front of a blazer, coat, or jacket that is typically an extension of the collar and stretches down the front side, along the neckline.

LOGO A design used by a brand to help the public identify its products, method, style, etc.

LUXURY Having a high level of quality, high prices, and exclusivity.

MAISON DE COUTURE A fashion house.

MATTE Smooth even surface made without shine.

MILLINER A person who makes and sells women's hats.

MINIMALIST A person who uses a small number of garments and accessories to complete an ensemble.

MODERNISM A movement in the 19th century that aimed to go against and break traditional standards by creating new ways of thinking in the art world.

MOJO A magnetic quality that attracts people to a person, place, or object.

MONOFILAMENT A single strand of fiber.

MOTIF A repeating element in a design.

PALETTE A group of colors, no more than six, that mesh well together and provide options when pairing colors in a wardrobe.

PETTICOAT An undergarment or underskirt worn under a skirt or dress.

PLEATED Folds in fabric used to create volume.

PRÊT-À-PORTER A designer who makes ready-to-wear fashion rather than made-to-measure.

READY-TO-WEAR Clothing made in standard sizes and intended to be purchased and worn off the rack, without alterations.

REPURPOSED The reuse of existing garments and materials into completely new designs with minimal use of new materials.

RUNWAY A long, and sometimes narrow structure used in fashion shows for models to display clothing to buyers and media.

SALON An establishment meant for a brand or designer to display and sell clothing currently available to the public.

SCULPTURAL GARMENT Garments that outline and exaggerate the natural curves to achieve a silhouette that can be recognized from every angle.

SECOND SKIN Clothing that fits closely to the skin and hugs the body tightly in an effort to define its natural curves.

SKETCH An unfinished drawing that lays out the foundation of an idea.

STREETWEAR Fashionable yet casual clothing.

SUSTAINABLE FASHION Clothing that is made of biodegradable materials and reduces the carbon footprint of the brand.

TAFFETA A crisp and shiny fabric made from a combination of synthetic fibers and considered the ideal material used to create ball gowns, wedding gowns, and high fashion evening wear.

TAPESTRY A heavy woven piece of fabric usually decorated with designs or images and used to hang on walls and cover furniture.

TEXTILE Any material that is created by interlacing (weaving, knitting, etc.) fibers.

TRADEMARK Legal protection of a brand or company's logo that prohibits its use by another organization.

TULLE A lightweight sheer fabric that, depending on the fiber it is made from, can be either stiff or soft with more flow. It is also often used for formal gowns and bridal wear.

ULTRASUEDE A machine washable fabric popularized by Halston in the 1970s. The fabric has a soft touch and was used to create functional clothing and travel wardrobe due to its versatility.

VISIONARY A person who has unique and broad ideas about what the future of an industry can become.

LCCN: 2023905988
ISBN: 978-1-9519631-5-6

Printed and bound in China
First printing, 2023